Text by Sophie Piper
Illustrations copyright © 2007 Sophy Williams
This edition copyright © 2012 Lion Hudson

The moral rights of the author and illustrator
have been asserted

A Lion Children's Book
an imprint of
Lion Hudson plc
Wilkinson House, Jordan Hill Road,
Oxford OX2 8DR, England
www.lionhudson.com
ISBN 978 0 7459 6291 7

First edition 2012
1 3 5 7 9 10 8 6 4 2 0

A catalogue record for this book is available
from the British Library

Typeset in 15/19 Lapidary 333 BT
Printed in China July 2012 (manufacturer LH17)

Distributed by:
UK: Marston Book Services Ltd, PO Box 269, Abingdon, Oxon OX14 4YN
USA: Trafalgar Square Publishing, 814 N Franklin Street, Chicago, IL 60610
USA Christian Market: Kregel Publications, PO Box 2607, Grand Rapids, MI 49501

The Child of Christmas

Retold by Sophie Piper
Illustrated by Sophy Williams

LION
CHILDREN'S

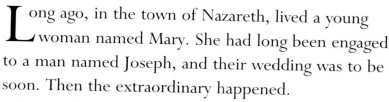

Long ago, in the town of Nazareth, lived a young woman named Mary. She had long been engaged to a man named Joseph, and their wedding was to be soon. Then the extraordinary happened.

An angel appeared to Mary and said, "Peace be with you. The Lord is with you and has greatly blessed you."

Mary was startled. What was happening? What did it mean?

"Do not be afraid," said the angel. "God has chosen you to be the mother of a child. You will name him Jesus. He will be known as the Son of God. His kingdom will never end."

Mary shook her head. "I'm not yet married," she said. "How can this happen to me?"

"Because of God's power," replied the angel simply. "There is nothing God cannot do."

Mary bowed her head. "I will do as God wants," she replied.

When Joseph found out that Mary was expecting a baby, he was dismayed.

"I'm not the baby's father," he sighed to himself. "How can it be right for me to be Mary's husband?

"I don't really have a choice: I shall have to break off the engagement. But when I do, Mary could so easily become the victim of unkind gossip. Oh dear... I shall have to find a way to sort everything out quietly."

While Joseph was thinking about all these things, an angel spoke to him in a dream.

"Joseph, do not be afraid to make Mary your wife. The child she bears is God's Son. You will name him Jesus, for he is the one God has chosen to save his people."

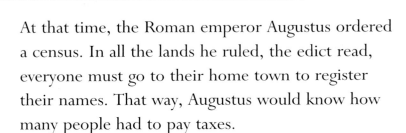

At that time, the Roman emperor Augustus ordered a census. In all the lands he ruled, the edict read, everyone must go to their home town to register their names. That way, Augustus would know how many people had to pay taxes.

Now, Joseph could trace his family line all the way back to the greatest king his people had ever had: King David, born in Bethlehem and once a humble shepherd boy. So it was to that town that Joseph and Mary went to register their names.

But of course, many other people were making similar journeys. When Mary and Joseph arrived in Bethlehem, there was no room in the inn. The only shelter they could find was a stable.

In that humble room, Mary's baby was born.

On a nearby hillside, some shepherds were out looking after their flocks. It was a dark night, but they knew the place well: the rocks and the thorn bushes around them, the starlit dome of the sky above.

It was a place where they could give voice to their grumbles without any fear of being heard: about the emperor's census, and the near certainty of an increase in taxes; about the Roman occupation and the everyday rudeness of the Roman soldiers who patrolled the streets; about cruel King Herod and whether or not his desire to stay in power was verging on insanity.

"What we need," they agreed, "is a king who is one of our people.

"A king like David of long ago, who will defeat all our enemies."

Out of the dark, an angel of God appeared and the whole place was lit with the glory of heaven.

"Don't be afraid," cried the angel. "I come with good news – news that will bring joy to the world.

"Tonight, in Bethlehem, your Saviour has been born. He is God's chosen king – Christ the Lord.

"This is how you will know that my words are true: you will find the baby wrapped in swaddling clothes and lying in a manger."

Suddenly a host of angels appeared in the sky, all singing:

"All glory be to God in heaven
And peace on earth below.
Tonight is born the Saviour
Who was promised long ago."

Then the angels vanished into heaven and the sky was dark again. The shepherds glanced at one another, unsure.

"Well, let's go to Bethlehem and see!" exclaimed one. "Let's find out for ourselves if what the angel said is true."

Together they hurried off along the paths they trod each day... along the streets they knew so well, to where a lamp shone from inside a stable.

They peered inside, and saw Joseph and Mary – and the baby lying in the manger.

Then they just had to burst in to tell them what the angel had said about the child. Mary listened intently, trying to remember every word.

From far away, others were also journeying towards Bethlehem.

In a country to the east, wise men had gathered to marvel at the appearance of a new star.

"It is surely the sign of a royal birth," they agreed; "a new king of the Jewish people."

So they had set out for Jerusalem, the great city where the Jews had built their Temple; the same city where a cruel king now ruled the people on behalf of his Roman overlords.

News of the foreigners and their quest reached King Herod, and he was not pleased.

He called for the priests and others who advised him on matters of religion.

"I know that the Jewish scriptures speak of a king who is to come," he said. "Where do they say this messiah will be born?"

"In Bethlehem," came the swift reply. "It is here, in the book of the prophet Micah."

King Herod dismissed the priests and scowled at his servants. "The foreigners who sparked these rumours of a newborn king — bring them here," he said, "secretly."

Later, by the flickering lamplight, King Herod listened to what the wise men had to say. He, in turn, sent them to Bethlehem.

"When you find the child, come back and tell me where he is," he said. "I too will go and worship him."

The wise men set off. It is not far from Jerusalem to Bethlehem, and the star they had seen in the east now lit their way.

It shone right over the place where the child was.

When they went inside and saw Jesus with his mother Mary, they knelt down to worship him.

Then they brought out rich gifts – gold, frankincense, and myrrh, and presented them, knowing they had found the newborn king.

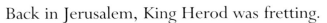

Back in Jerusalem, King Herod was fretting.

The people he ruled were only too eager to be free of Roman rule. They dreamed of a king who would set them free. Rumours that God's messiah had come would make them rebellious… And then what would become of Herod and the power he had fought so hard to wield?

When those foreigners returned, he would deal with the child as he had dealt with other rivals: with a murderous plan.

But the foreigners did not return. In a dream, an angel warned them.

"Do not go back to Herod. Return to your own country by a different road."

After they had gone, an angel appeared in Joseph's dream.

"King Herod will soon come looking for the child," said the angel. "Get up — take Jesus and Mary to a place of safety.

"Go to Egypt, and stay there until I tell you to leave."

So the little family made their way, protected by God's own angels.

For Jesus was born to be king, and his kingdom must never end.